D0557316

HOME
THE FINAL FRONTIER

Other Close to Home Books
by John McPherson

Close to Home
One Step Closer to Home
Dangerously Close to Home

Treasury Collection
Close to Home Revisited

Also from John McPherson

High School Isn't Pretty
Close to Home: A Book of Postcards

HOME
THE FINAL FRONTIER

A CLOSE TO HOME
COLLECTION

BY JOHN McPHERSON

Andrews and McMeel
A Universal Press Syndicate Company
Kansas City

Close to Home is distributed internationally by Universal Press Syndicate.

Home: The Final Frontier copyright © 1996 by John McPherson. All rights reserved. Printed in the United States of America. No part of this book may be used or reproduced in any manner whatsoever without written permission except in the case of reprints in the context of reviews. For information write Andrews and McMeel, a Universal Press Syndicate Company, 4520 Main Street, Kansas City, Missouri 64111.

ISBN: 0-8362-1030-1

Library of Congress Catalog Card Number: 95-83541

First Printing, March 1996
Second Printing, September 1996

ATTENTION: SCHOOLS AND BUSINESSES

Andrews and McMeel books are available at quantity discounts with bulk purchase for educational, business, or sales promotional use. For information, write to: Special Sales Department, Andrews and McMeel, 4520 Main Street, Kansas City, Missouri 64111.

For Chris Lutes

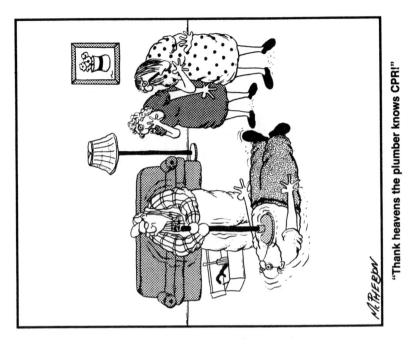

"Thank heavens the plumber knows CPR!"

"Now's the part where you're supposed to say,
'The important thing is that you're OK, son.' Give it
a try, Dad. Eight simple words."

"I think your serve would improve significantly if you'd just get that thing restrung."

"Next, attach shunt C to rod F'... Hey, wait! These are the assembly instructions for the kids' swing set, not the tent."

Since it was a gift from Carla, Vern felt obligated to wear his deodorant-on-a-rope to work the next day.

"Those maniacs up in 4-C are growing watermelons in their window box again this year."

"Before we begin today's dissection lab,
I'd like you each to select your lab specimen
and take it back to your lab table."

"All I did was hit the delete button!"

"In addition to the stereo, this one's also got AC."

"Here's your allowance. You're free to do with it as you please, but I strongly recommend that you put 25 percent of it away for retirement."

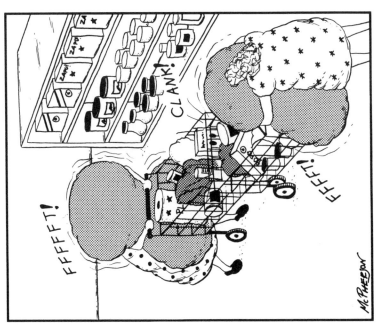

Fortunately for Donna and Clarice, Food Wizard had the foresight to install airbags in its shopping carts.

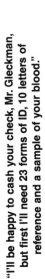

"I'll be happy to cash your check, Mr. Gleckman, but first I'll need 23 forms of ID, 10 letters of reference and a sample of your blood."

The Bowman Paint Co. needed to work on coming up with more appealing names for its paint shades.

"I think we better have a little talk with Wilson after the meet."

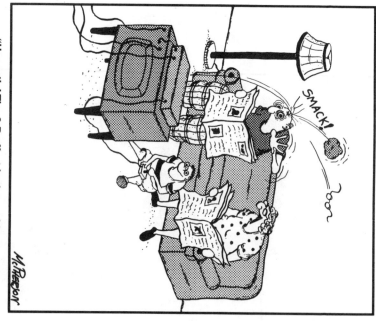

"Honestly! The 3-D effect in these video games is incredible!"

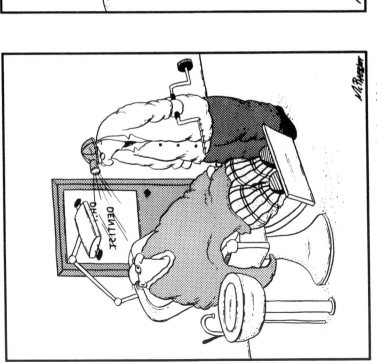

"You've probably noticed that we're in the midst of a power outage here."

"Worst slice I ever saw!"

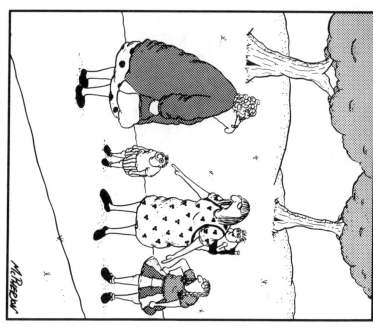

"The baby is four months, Jason is 17 months, and Lisa is 147 months."

"All right! All right! We can get a dishwasher!"

"If you paid $5,300 for an exclusive deep-sea fishing excursion and spent the entire time seasick in the bathroom, you'd probably mount the bait bucket, too."

"Some joker sprayed the melons again with that hair-in-a-can stuff."

"Quick! Put this Nixon mask on the Simkins baby! His father's coming down the hall!"

"... FOR MR. MORRISON'S ANSWERING MACHINE, PRESS 76. FOR MR. FRAWLEY'S ANSWERING MACHINE, PRESS 77. IF FOR SOME REASON YOU NEED TO SPEAK TO AN ACTUAL HUMAN, PLEASE CALL ON THE THIRD FRIDAY OF THE MONTH BETWEEN 8:12 A.M. AND 8:29 A.M. EASTERN TIME."

COSMETICS

"You've got two options. You can wait until a technician from the escalator company files in here on Monday, or we can start it up and hope that you come out at the top."

"Management says they're fed up with losing foul balls and homers to the fans."

"Which do you want? Fudge Royale or Neapolitan?"

"When was the last time we dusted around here?"

Successful executives know the importance of unwinding after a high-pressure meeting.

"Claudia, you've come to the right place. Our firm specializes in hair salon malpractice suits."

"This workout tape's a little more laid-back than some of the others."

The city's new parking meters, which spew hot tar onto cars whose time has expired, proved to be highly effective battling scofflaws.

"Sorry, sir, we're out of boxes."

Thanks to the wonders of virtual reality,
fathers can now completely experience
the miracle of giving birth.

"And you're *sure* you had the door when you entered?"

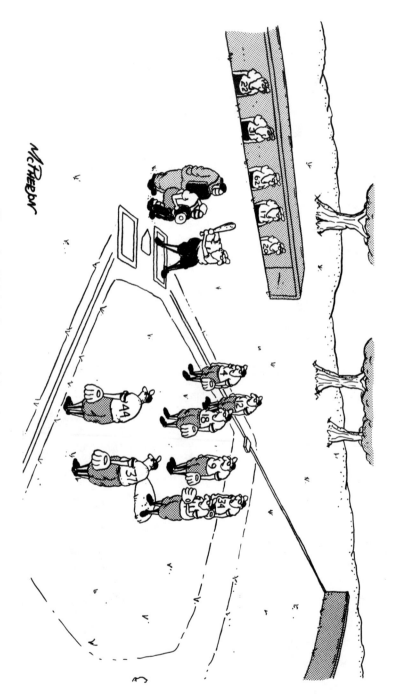

Wayne's .026 batting average was well-known throughout the league.

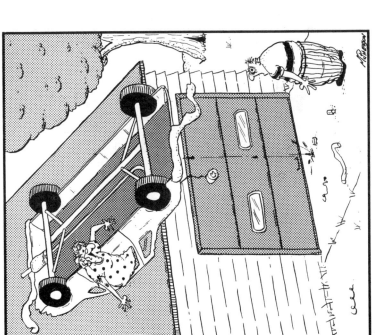

"I still haven't quite gotten used to the clutch on this car."

"My dog ate it."

Some shoppers felt that Zippy Grocery Stores had gone too far with this latest offering of free samples.

"Comstock's moving a little slow on that Megatron Industries proposal. Give him 75 volts for five seconds. What the heck, make that 10 seconds."

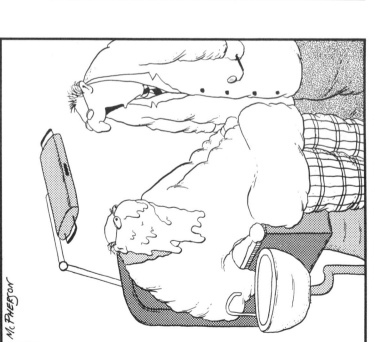

"That Novocain should wear off in two or three days."

What not to say to your wife when she's in labor.

"That 'jerk' that keeps trying to pass us is our trailer."

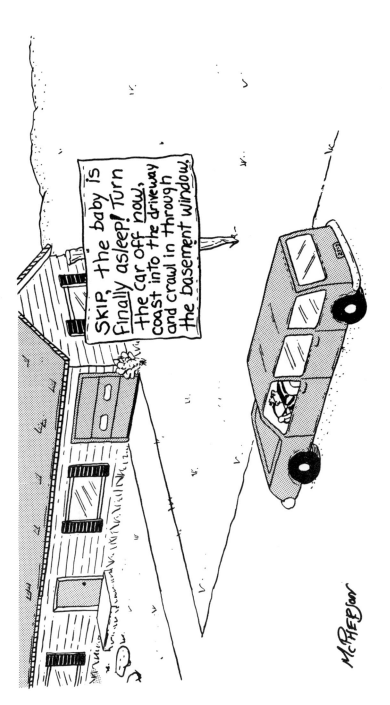

"Hey, Bert. There's a woman here who wants to know if we offer memberships."

"This new massage showerhead you installed gives me the creeps!"

"It's a version of the old shell game. The nurse shuffles the babies around and you bet on which one is yours. So far I've lost 40 bucks."

"He's a real lap cat, that one is!"

"The earpiece on the phone was starting to look pretty gross."

"This? Oh, nothing. It's just a radio-transmitter collar so Lisa's dad can track you down if you don't get her home by midnight. No big deal."

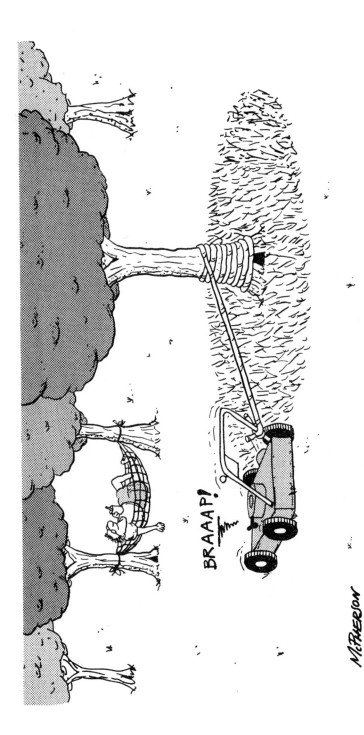

Bud Wellman discovers the true value of a self-propelled lawn mower.

Hoping to appeal to both performance-minded dads and practical moms, Chevrolet develops the Corvette minivan.

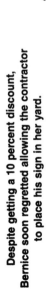

Despite getting a 10 percent discount,
Bernice soon regretted allowing the contractor
to place his sign in her yard.

Management trainee J. K. Boodley tests the
boundaries of the company's new dress code.

"I've got her in one of those new 24-hour diapers."

A typical group photo taken with an auto-timer.

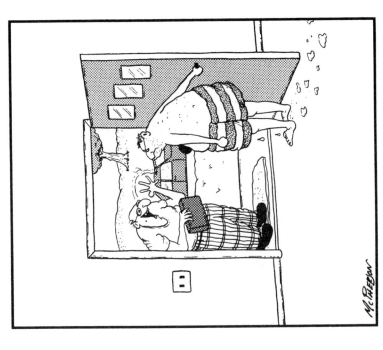

"Good evening, sir! I was on my way to the video store and realized I forgot to rewind the tape. Mind if I use your VCR?"

"Kathy! Kathy! Snap out of it! Your aerobics show has been over for 20 minutes! That's 'Mister Rogers' Neighborhood' you're watching!"

"Buying that mirror from the funhouse was the smartest thing we ever did."

Knowing that he was about to be fired,
Vern took the company car out for one last spin.

45

"Oh, that? That's so I can keep your socks paired up in the laundry."

Hoping to smooth over the heated dispute he had had with Mr. Grant, Ron breaks into the Barney theme song.

Fortunately for the rest of the family, the camcorder's boredom sensor kicked in after Dan had spent 10 minutes filming the baby sucking on her toe.

"If it bothers you, tell him to put his feet down! Otherwise, quit whining to me about it!"

"You bonehead! That's the same lamp we sold at our garage sale last year for $3!"

SPLAT!

"Children or non-children?"

A definite sign that you'll be waiting for your doctor's appointment much longer than expected.

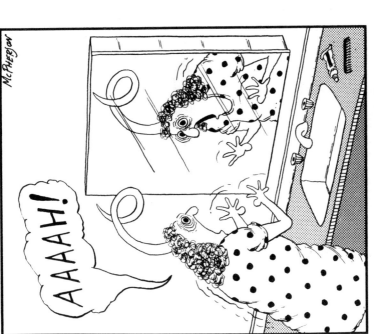

AAAAH!

Although she had had a few gray hairs in the past, Kay found this one particularly hard to accept.

"The moles have been just *awful* this year!"

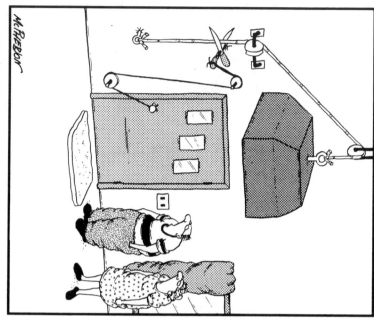

"For $1,800 I expected our home security system to be a little more sophisticated than this!"

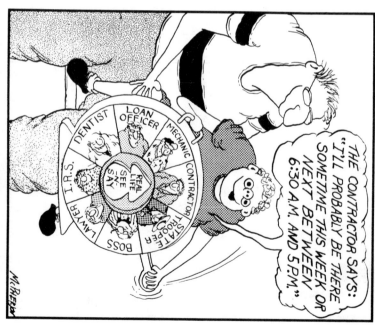

THE CONTRACTOR SAYS: "I'LL PROBABLY BE THERE SOMETIME THIS WEEK OR NEXT BETWEEN 6:30 A.M. AND 5 P.M."

One of many new toys designed to help children learn more about the real world.

Edwin's new Eau de Hershey Bar cologne was
having a dramatic effect on his love life.

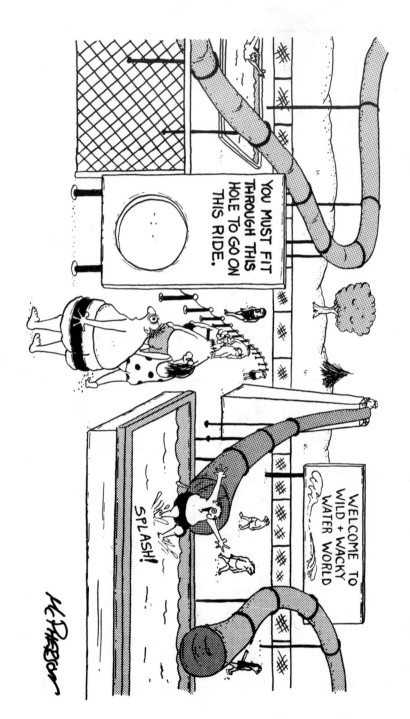

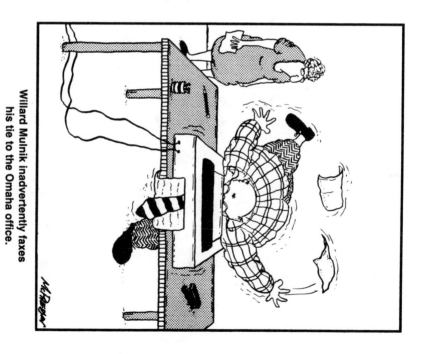

Willard Mulnik inadvertently faxes
his tie to the Omaha office.

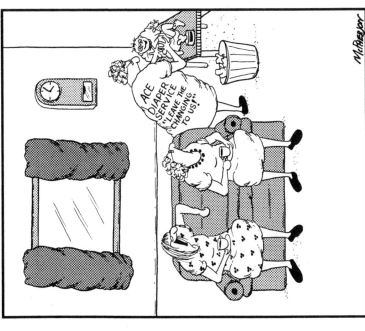

Carl wore the slippers for two weeks until one day they had an unfortunate "accident" involving the garbage disposal.

"This diaper service is 30 bucks more a week than any of the others, but it's well worth it."

"Look, it's nothing personal. I just can't handle
your cold feet any longer."

"Hold still! I want to use up these last few shots on the roll!"

"Hold it! Nobody move! I just lost a contact!"

"He must smell your cat."

Having narrowed the field of candidates to three, personnel goes through the final selection process.

"Does anybody have a one-inch hex nut?!!"

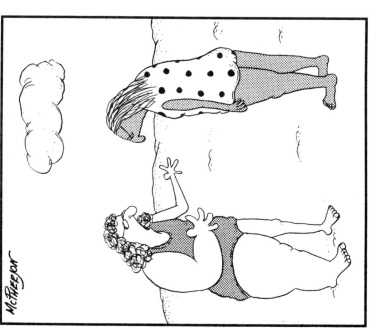

"So, to make a long story short, the insurance company tells us in the midst of it all that it'll pay for only half of the liposuction."

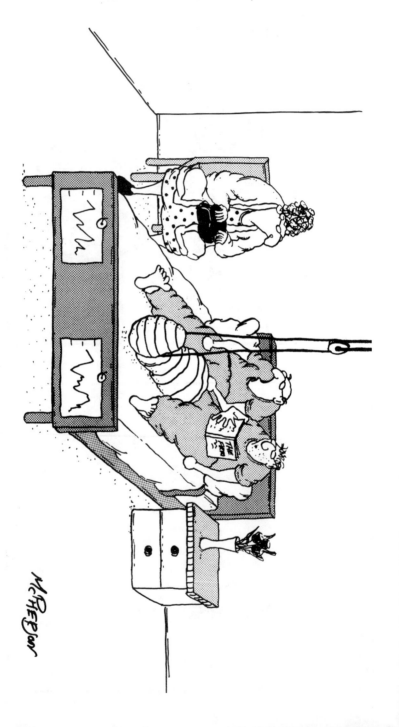

"I know I asked for an economy room, but this is ridiculous."

In a play unprecedented in league history, Ned Felmley misreads the third-base coach's signals and steals the pitcher's mound.

"We gotta stop feeding the dog dry food."

With any luck, maintenance would take the hint
and turn down the air conditioning.

The new breed of insensitive friends:
People who call during "Seinfeld."

"He's at the stage now where everything he gets
his hands on goes straight into his mouth."

More and more businesses are teaming up
with airlines to offer frequent-flier miles
to their customers.

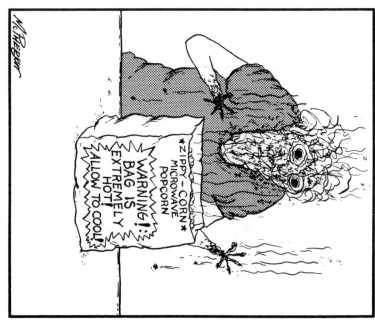

The leading cause of injuries in the home.

"Something tells me the dog resents having been trained to retrieve the paper."

"For heaven's sake! All he wants to do is play horsey with his dad!
Will you stop whimpering and at least *try*
to jump over the coffee table?!"

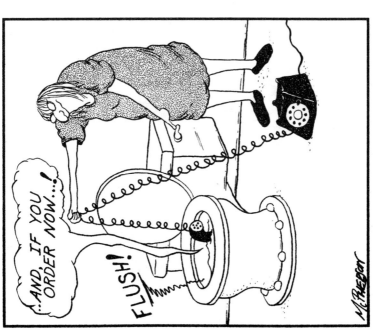

Sheila had an effective way of letting
telemarketers know she wasn't interested.

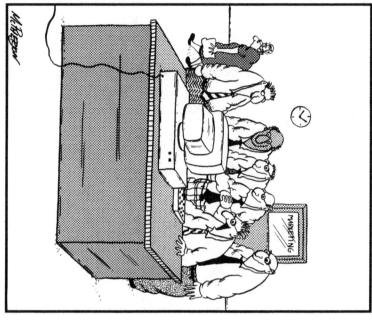

"By adding a new 120-megabyte hard drive and using the software that Ed developed over the last six months, we can compute anybody's handicap to within 1/1,000th of a stroke."

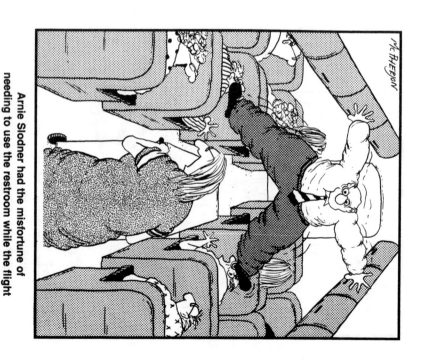

Arnie Slodner had the misfortune of needing to use the restroom while the flight attendants were serving beverages.

"Cotton candy? You traded your *glove* for some cotton candy?!!"

Thanks to their new garage-sale detector, Norma and Darlene hit a record 11 garage sales in one hour.

In an attempt to get their patients to relax more, many dentists have installed Jacuzzis in their offices.

When wedding photographers abuse their power.

Bobby's excitement about going to summer camp faded as soon as he read the sign.

"Take one of these every time you inhale."

"I don't think the chemicals in those flea dips are good for him."

"You rode your bike to work again, didn't you?"

"Something tells me that the guy in the room above me isn't doing so well."

At the Department of Motor Vehicles Employee Training Center.

"Our dryer's broken."

"Go get the phone number of those idiots who installed the vinyl siding."

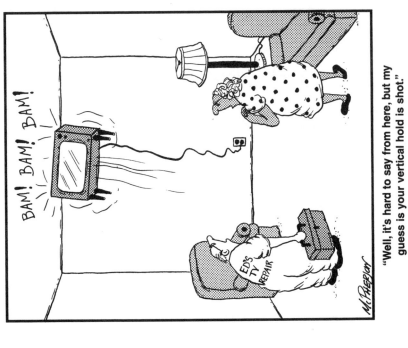

"Well, it's hard to say from here, but my guess is your vertical hold is shot."

"Here's one that says 'Pat Frawley' on it. Pat Frawley hasn't worked here since 1987!"

"Well, this is a first. He swallowed one of my gloves!"

How to tell when it's time to clean up your driveway.

Ed Mosberg's cannonball would go down in Pulver Country Club history.

Wendy and Charlene were pretty impressed with
Ed's surfing abilities until the tide receded.

"Well, your lawn's all set, Mrs. Fertstein! Here are some hermetically sealed protective suits and some respirators in case someone actually needs to walk on the lawn this summer."

MCPHEELOR

"We should've bought one of those cardboard shades to put on the dashboard."

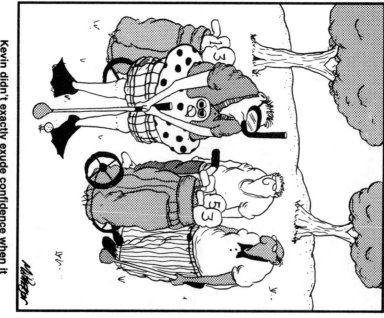

Kevin didn't exactly exude confidence when it came to driving over water hazards.

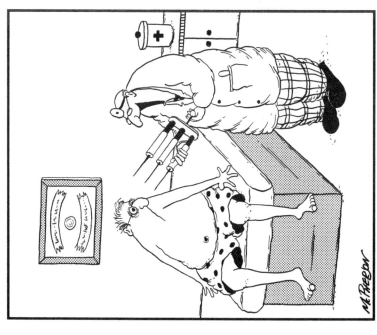

"Fortunately, medical researchers have been able to combine tetanus, smallpox and rubella vaccinations into one shot."

"So, how's the rototilling going, Mr. I-Don't-Need-to-Read-the Directions?"

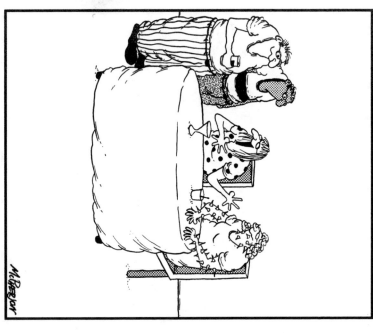

"I'm Carla and this is my friend Rose."

LUGGAGE COMPACTOR TS-4900

KACHUNG!

"If you ask me, the neighbors are abusing this new leash law."

Lois Mulner wanted to make sure nobody walked off with her bag by mistake.

BAGGAGE CLAIM AREA

"Nice break!"

Accurately ordering mulch by the cubic
yard is a skill that few people possess.

"Oh, for heaven's sake! This one doesn't feel right either!"

"I had trouble reading your doctor's handwriting, but I think I figured it out. However, if you start to drool uncontrollably or gain more than 15 pounds in a week, stop taking them."

"Here's today's special: braised beef medallions in a sherry sauce. I'm sure this kind gentleman won't mind if you all sample a bite."

"I just figured, hey, why spend a fortune on a set of yuppie-looking wrist and ankle weights?"

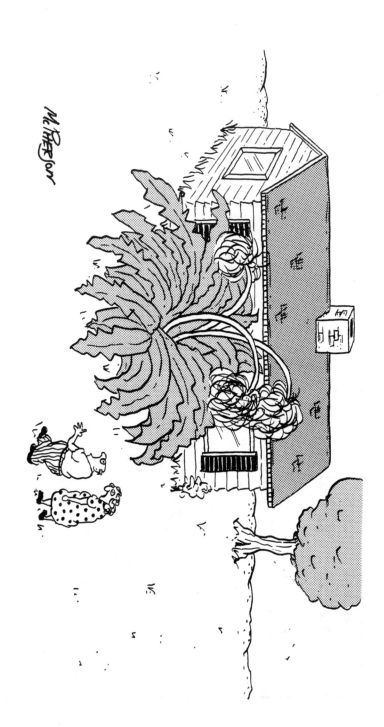

"Well, look on the bright side.
It's the only weed in the whole yard."

"Are you *serious?!* She won't let you take off the shirt until *all* of those chores are done?!"

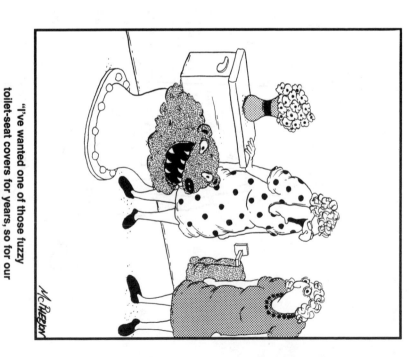

"Well now, Mr. Fenderson, what seems to be the problem?"

DR. T. BIMSFORD
CHIROPRACTOR

"I've wanted one of those fuzzy toilet-seat covers for years, so for our 40th anniversary Earl went all out!"

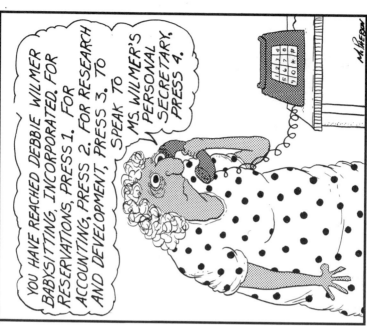

A clear sign that your baby sitter is becoming too popular.

When it got right down to it, nobody had time to spend drying his hands under the new electric hand dryer.

A good indication that the softball league you've joined isn't overly competitive.

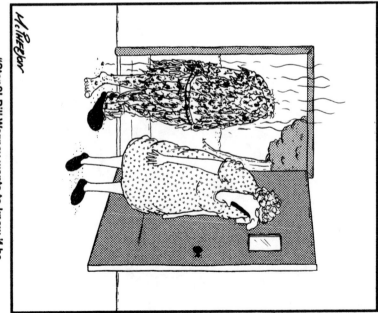

"Stan?! Bill Wazney wants to know if he can borrow our fire extinguisher!"

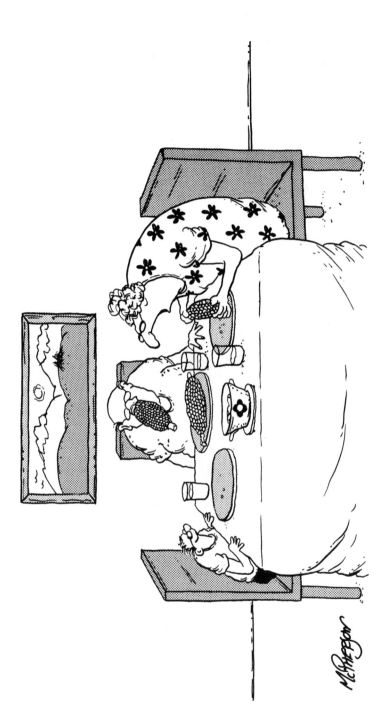

"Don't play with your food, dear."

"When the guy at the front desk told us there was a bar in our room, this wasn't what I had in mind."

Without a doubt, one of the all-time
worst places to get a flat.

Day-care centers are becoming
increasingly selective about which
students they admit for enrollment.

"He fell while he was trying to install some of those nonslip decals in the tub."

Vern was starting to sense that Sheila's interest in him was fading.

Some of the rides at the Fernvale County Fair left a lot to be desired.

"And here are the keys to the car."

"Hey, I agree with you! They did a great job cleaning the carpets. I just think they should've asked before they stenciled their logo on the rug!"

For people who can't afford a minivan, elastic trunk lids are proving to be an inexpensive alternative.

In an effort to prepare expectant parents for the challenges that lie ahead, many obstetricians' offices have installed parenthood simulators.

PARENTHOOD SIMULATOR

● ON
○ OFF

SETTING   ■ TURBO

● 2 A.M. FEEDING
● LOST PACIFIER
● CHICKEN POX
● WET BED
● TERRIBLE TWOS
● COLICKY BABY
● COLICKY TRIPLETS
● PROJECTILE VOMITING
● UNSOLICITED ADVICE

"I'm sorry, sir, but leg room is no longer a service that we offer to our coach passengers."

"These pills come with a child-proof cap, but as an added precaution they're manufactured to look exactly like lima beans."

"For her 12 years of service as a data processor and for keypunching in 3,789 records in one eight-hour shift, please welcome our employee of the year, Peggy Neal!"

The Wassermans discover that the air bags in their new car are a tad on the sensitive side.

"What kind of an idiot drinks three cups of coffee after 9 p.m.?!"

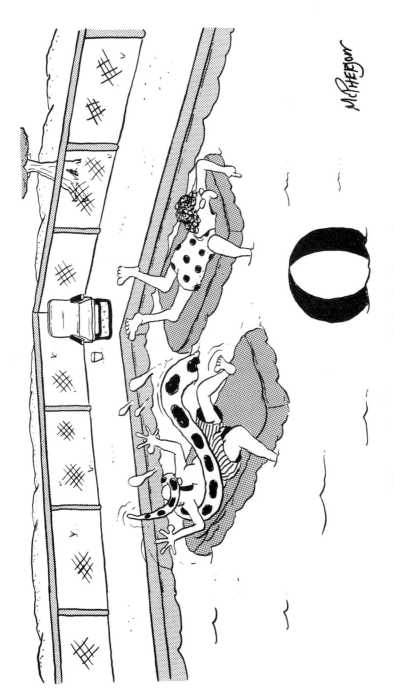

"We need to put more chlorine in the pool.
I think I see some algae growing here."

"Hi! We're the Litmans! We tried to rent *Jurassic Park* but were told that you folks got the last copy. Mind if we watch it with you?"

"Unbelievable! What are the chances of *three* drill bits snapping off in a row like that?!"

"Oh, I forgot to tell you. I let the kids take the spare tire to play with in the sandbox."

"That goofball over there offered me five bucks to put this helmet on his kid long enough to get a photo."

"It's a free trial-size sample of cat litter."

Dwayne was starting to reconsider his decision to be water boy for the cross-country team.

The real reason Al Brimlow bought a mulching mower.

"OK, hit the button!"

The management at Chandler Industries didn't have much tact when it came to layoffs.

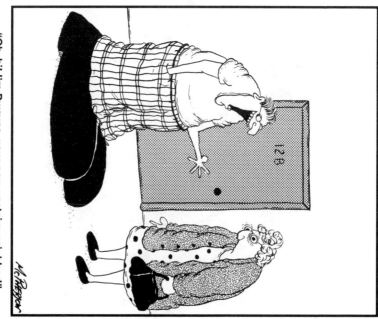

"Oh, hi! I'm Dwayne, your new upstairs neighbor!"

Although all of the players were given uniforms,
it didn't take long to figure out which guys
weren't going to make the final cut.

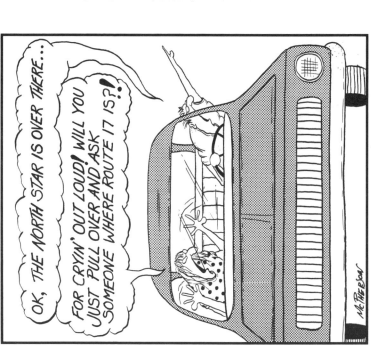

"We have no idea what you have, Mr. Schaad, but whatever it is, it's extremely contagious."

As a service to health-conscious customers, many grocery stores have installed scanners that calculate the total number of calories purchased.

The Wormsleys had had one too many milkshakes
spilled on their new cloth seats.

Unable to afford bells for a bell choir, members of the Maple Valley Church improvised as best they could.

Dwayne made a mental note to change the filter in the furnace.

Even though he hadn't asked to have his hair cut, Dave felt obligated to pay the street-corner barber.

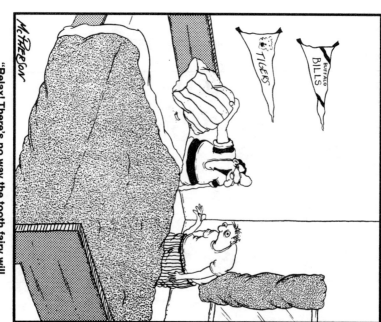

"Relax! There's no way the tooth fairy will figure out that they're dog teeth!"

"There must've been a hundred signs!
'Don't Feed the Bears'! So what do you?!
You start handing cookies to them!"

Vera's desire to slim down for her honeymoon
was turning into a full-scale obsession.

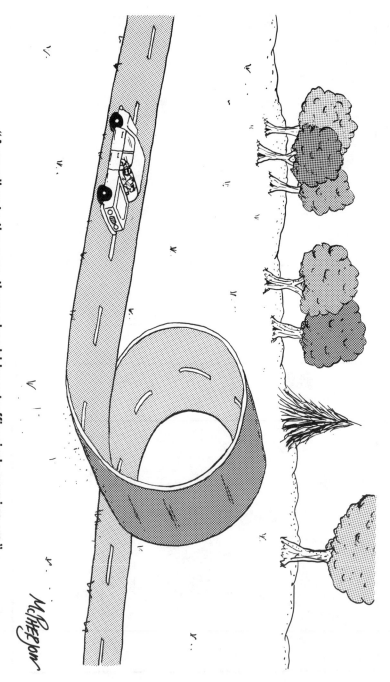

"According to the map, there should be a traffic circle coming up."

This incident, involving the neighbors' *Sunday Times Herald*, forced Lois to admit that she had a coupon-clipping addiction.

Dwight was having a difficult time accepting the fact that summer was over.

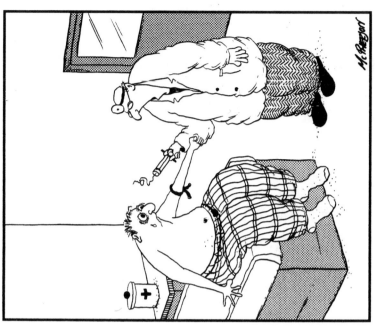

"Don't clench your fist quite so hard."

Twenty-seven weeks on the all-radish diet
finally pushed Carolyn over the edge.

MICROBIOLOGY
MR. LURWAD

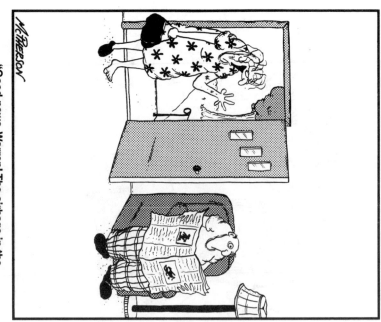

"Good news, Warren! The airbags in the
new car work perfectly!"